Post-Truth Rhetoric
and Composition

Post-Truth Rhetoric and Composition

Bruce McComiskey

Current Arguments in Composition

Utah State University Press
Logan

© 2017 by University Press of Colorado

All rights reserved
Published by Utah State University Press
An imprint of University Press of Colorado
5589 Arapahoe Avenue, Suite 206C
Boulder, Colorado 80303

 The University Press of Colorado is a proud member of
The Association of American University Presses.

The University Press of Colorado is a cooperative publishing enterprise supported,
in part, by Adams State University, Colorado State University, Fort
Lewis College, Metropolitan State University of Denver, Regis University,
University of Colorado, University of Northern Colorado, Utah State
University, and Western State Colorado University.

USU Press Current Arguments in Composition

DOI: 10.7330/9781607327455
ISBN 978-1-60732-744-8 (pbk.: alk. paper)
E-ISBN 978-1-60732-745-5 (e-book)

Library of Congress Cataloging-in-Publication Data

Names: McComiskey, Bruce, 1963– author.
Title: Post-truth rhetoric and composition / Bruce McComiskey.
Description: Logan : Utah State University Press, [2017] | Includes
    bibliographical references.
Identifiers: LCCN 2017023340| ISBN 9781607327448 (pbk.) | ISBN
    9781607327455 (ebook)
Subjects: LCSH: Presidents—United States—Election—2016. | Truthfulness
    and falsehood—Political aspects—United States—History—21st century.
    | Rhetoric—Political aspects—United States—History—21st century. |
    Communication in politics—United States—History—21st century. | English
    language—Rhetoric—Study and teaching (Higher)—United States.
Classification: LCC E911 .M39 2017 | DDC 324.973/0905—dc23
LC record available at https://lccn.loc.gov/2017023340

Contents

Post-Truth Rhetoric
and Composition

Post-Truth Rhetoric and Composition

On November 8, 2016, the United States of America elected real estate mogul Donald J. Trump to be its forty-fifth president. Trump did not win this election in the usual way, with an occasional negative ad but in general using sincere argumentation and ethical persuasion in order to demonstrate that he has the most relevant experience and the best plan to move the country forward. Instead, Trump won the election using unethical rhetorical strategies like alt-right fake news, vague social media posts, policy reversals, denials of meaning, attacks on media credibility, name-calling, and so on. All of these unethical rhetorical strategies, constantly televised and repeated throughout the year-long campaign and election cycle, have deeply affected public discourse in general, not just Trump's personal use of it. The Southern Poverty Law Center and others call this negative influence of Trump's rhetoric on social institutions and cultural interactions "the Trump effect," or a generalized increase in violence and hatred throughout the country.

Trump's campaign and election represent a rhetorical watershed moment in two ways: first, there has been a shift in the way that powerful people use unethical rhetoric to accomplish their goals; and, second, there has been a shift in the way that public audiences consume unethical rhetoric. Not surprisingly, the organizations that are most committed to promoting

and teaching ethical rhetoric and writing have viewed this rhetorical watershed moment as a direct challenge to their missions
and as an exigence for calls to rhetorical action.

On November 21, 2016, Gregory Clark, president of the
Rhetoric Society of America (RSA), emailed a message to all
RSA members on the organization's listserv, and this message
was subsequently posted on the RSA website.[1] In this statement,
Clark identifies the rancorous election as a powerful exigence
for an ethical response. Clark's response to this rancor, which
was also rhetorically successful (resulting in Trump's election),
emphasizes RSA's core values: diversity, inclusion, and respect.
The very fact that Clark felt the need to reaffirm these values
signifies a certain anxiety that Trump's successful rhetoric represents a direct challenge to RSA and its rhetorical mission.

On the very next day, November 22, 2016, Susan Miller-
Cochran, president of the Council of Writing Program
Administrators (CWPA), sent a message over the WPA-L listserv, reaffirming that organization's core values and condemn-
ing the negative rhetorical strategies that were so divisive and so
successful throughout the 2016 campaign and election process.[2]
The CWPA statement is similar to the RSA statement since it
reinforces CWPA's core values—diversity and inclusiveness—
in the wake of a campaign that succeeded by exploiting latent
xenophobia. The CWPA statement is different from the RSA
statement, however, since it directly condemns institutional-
ized inequality, and it calls upon its members to "explicitly act
against the structures that cause injustice today." The CWPA
statement is a call to rhetorical arms. The exigence of this statement (like RSA's) is a general anxiety among writing teachers
that their core values have been called into question, and the
intent of the statement is to reinforce support for any action
writing teachers and program administrators might take to

oppose the unethical rhetorical values that were so successful in the 2016 election.

A couple of weeks later, on December 6, 2016, the weekly *NCTE Inbox* email, sent to all members of the National Council of Teachers of English (NCTE), contained a link to a new statement from the Conference on College Composition and Communication (CCCC), the "Statement on Language, Power, and Action."[3] Like the other statements, the CCCC statement reinforces the core values of the organization: the power of language, commitment to diversity and justice, responsible inquiry, and ethical communication. The same general anxiety that fuels the RSA and CWPA statements also fuels the CCCC statement—demeaning and disempowering, though ultimately successful, rhetoric and writing. Although the CCCC statement does not directly promote action against oppressive institutional forces (like the CWPA statement does), the CCCC statement is clear that language is powerful and must be used and taught responsibly, not just strategically, with the intent to win at all costs.[4]

Although not one of these three institutional responses uses the term *post-truth*, it is clear that the rhetorical strategies associated with post-truth politics and rhetoric are at the heart of their exigence. In November 2016, Oxford Dictionaries announced *post-truth* as its word of the year. The Oxford Dictionaries web page defines *post-truth* as an adjective "relating to or denoting circumstances in which objective facts are less influential in shaping public opinion than appeals to emotion and personal belief." Although the word *post-truth* is not new, Oxford Dictionaries selected it as word of the year because of a "spike in frequency" following the UK's Brexit and the US presidential campaign and election.[5] During the past year, Oxford Dictionaries explains, "*Post-truth* has gone from being a peripheral term to being a mainstay in political commentary, now being used by major publications without the need for clarification or definition in their headlines." There is nothing post-truth about the word *post-truth*; it is a fact of life, it is here to stay, and, as rhetoricians and teachers of writing, we're going to have to deal with it.

In its current usage, *post-truth* signifies a state in which language lacks any reference to facts, truths, and realities. When language has no reference to facts, truths, or realities, it becomes a purely strategic medium. In a post-truth communication landscape, people (especially politicians) say whatever might work in a given situation, whatever might generate the desired result, without any regard to the truth value or facticity of statements. If a statement works, results in the desired effect, it is good; if it fails, it is bad (or at least not worth trying again). In *Post-Truth Rhetoric and Composition*, I describe the unethical rhetoric that has emerged in our post-truth world, and I discuss some of the consequences of post-truth rhetoric for composition studies. My intent is not to solve the problem of post-truth rhetoric, but only to define and describe it. We as a community of writing teachers will have to solve the problem of post-truth rhetoric collectively and over time.

POST-TRUTH RHETORIC

In their most powerful forms, rhetorics deal with sound arguments and reasoned opinions, not certain facts, foundational realities, or universal truths. When positivist science determines certain facts and foundational realities, and metaphysical philosophy reveals universal truths, there is not much work left for rhetoric to accomplish, other than to dress scientific facts and realities and philosophical truths in beautiful and persuasive words. However, the very notions of sound arguments and reasoned opinions require facts, realities, and truths as epistemological counterparts, as references and standards against which adjectives like "sound" and "reasoned" may be compared. Thus, all rhetorics (until very recently, that is) have existed on an epistemological continuum that includes certain facts, foundational realities, and universal truths, even when these rhetorics do not themselves participate in those facts, realities, and truths.

In Plato's works, for example, misleading sophistic rhetorics, bent on success, can only be understood as such within the context of an epistemological continuum that includes metaphysical truth and universal ethics. Sophistic rhetorics are misleading only in comparison to truth, which cannot mislead. In Aristotle, arguments and opinions can only be understood as sound and reasoned within the context of an epistemological continuum that includes truth and ethics. An argument is only sound and an opinion is only reasoned if it approaches (without reaching) truth on the epistemological continuum. More recently, Stephen Toulmin and Chaim Perelman and Lucie Olbrechts-Tyteca situate rhetoric within practical reasoning and against the foundational epistemological claims of philosophy and science. Practical reasoning can only be understood as such in relation to the universal claims of philosophy and science (i.e., reasoning is practical in part because it is not universal or abstract). Thus, probabilities, sound arguments, and reasoned opinions are understandable as such only because they can be plotted on an epistemological continuum that includes universal truth and foundational reality, even if the rhetorics that are based on contingent terms (probability, opinion) do not themselves participate in truth and reality.

Rhetoric has always dealt with unethical language in relation to an epistemological continuum that includes truth. Lies, fallacies, and doublespeak are recognized as false and unethical rhetorical strategies because they can be compared unfavorably to reasoned opinions and universal truths. Rhetors must *know the facts* in order to mislead through lies; they must *recognize the truth* in order to deceive through fallacies; and they must *understand reality* in order to manipulate through doublespeak. But what happens when facts, realities, and truths become overrated and disappear from the epistemological continuum? Without facts and realities as a reference or truths as a standard, then their opposites (lies, fallacies, and doublespeak) also disappear from the continuum. In this post-truth world (without truth *or* lies), language becomes purely strategic, without reference to anything other than itself. In this world without truth, a public description of sexual assault becomes "locker room talk" because that is what a powerful person calls it; a public expression of xenophobia becomes "telling it like it is" because ideologies dominated by fear suddenly find a voice; a public display of aggression and violence becomes "the enthusiasm factor" because ideological extremism will likely translate into votes.

The ultimate goal for the post-truth rhetor becomes, according to Benjamin Tallis (2016), "the destabilization or even the destruction of the notion of Truth as such" (8). Tallis explains that post-truth politicians "play to a widespread and increasingly cynical, anti-expert and supposedly anti-establishment and anti-authority mood, but one that clearly also still craves leadership and ambition" (9). And this epistemological and political cynicism is difficult to address rhetorically because it is not rooted in individual claims that can be challenged, but is instead rooted in larger ideological systems of belief that hold firm even when supporting claims are proven false. Tallis writes: "[C]orrecting the falsehoods of the post-truthers will never trump Trump or put Putin in the shade because it will not dissuade many people from 'believing' in the bigger, more compelling post-truths they offer. They offer people meaningful and attractive interpretations of their current condition and future possibilities, however far-fetched, factually incorrect, or empirically biased they may be" (10). While other politicians may be implicated in the rise of post-truth rhetoric, one single event has ushered in post-truth posthaste: "The election of Donald Trump has seen the flowering of the post-truth landscape" (Marcus 2016, A17).

Bullshit

Harry G. Frankfurt published his book *On Bullshit* in 2005 (which is actually a reprint of an essay he published earlier), well before Brexit and the rise of Trump, so it is unclear exactly what Frankfurt would have said about post-truth rhetoric today. But there is one thing about Frankfurt's discussion of bullshit that stands out in my mind: he disassociates bullshit from the epistemological continuum, thus relieving it of any reference to reality or responsibility to truth. Frankfurt writes that bullshit is "unconnected to a concern with the truth"; it "is not germane to the enterprise of describing reality"; and it proceeds "without any regard for how things really are" (Frankfurt 2005, 30). This is why Frankfurt says that bullshit "cannot be regarded as lying," because bullshitters do not "presume" to "know the truth" and thus cannot be accused of promoting a false position or describing a false reality (33).[6] Frankfurt writes, "The liar is inescapably concerned with truth-values" (51), while the bullshitter is not. According to Frankfurt, it is "this indifference to how things really are" that is "the essence of bullshit" (34). The bullshitter "does not care whether the things he says describe reality correctly. He just picks them out, or makes them up, to suit his purpose" (56). If that purpose happens to be victory in a party primary or presidential election, then the bullshitter will "not merely [be] producing one instance of bullshit; it involves a *program* of producing bullshit to whatever extent the circumstances require" (51). Since bullshit requires an indifference to reality or truth, "the statements people make [when bullshitting] do not necessarily reveal what they really believe or how they really feel" (36). Thus, bullshit is pure strategic communication with no reference to reality or truth. A candidate for party nomination or for president of the United States, for example, could pick a party line and say anything that is consistent with that ideological position while never worrying about speaking the truth.

James Fredal (2011) relates bullshit directly to the structures and purposes of rhetoric: "The parallel to the Aristotelian rhetorical triad is not accidental, for like rhetoric, bullshit presumes a speaker, a listener, and a text that enacts a symbolic exchange characteristic of language in use. Both rhetoric and bullshit attend to the power of speech, not only to shape and influence the speaker, the listener, their relationship, and their shared world, but to construct each of these elements from moment to moment through the ongoing negotiation of each encounter. And bullshit, like rhetoric, must emphasize the centrality of the response of the audience as the end of any given encounter" (245). And, later, Fredal says, "[A] full view of the phenomenon [of bullshit] would have to account for the interactional quality of bullshit, involving not only a speaker with a specific set of qualities or concerns (his or her intent or ethos), but also characteristic features of the bullshit itself (logos), and any resulting responses on the part of the audience or addressee (pathos), as well as the embeddedness of this interaction within the larger social drama" (247).[7] Later, I argue that in post-truth rhetoric, ethos and pathos function best at the expense of logos, but I appreciate Fredal's general argument that bullshit is rhetorical.

The intent of bullshit, or the rhetorical purpose of the bull-shitter, Fredal (2011) writes, is to deceive "listeners about his lack of concern for the truth" (245). Frankfurt explains, "Since bullshit need not be false, it differs from lies in its misrepre-sentational intent. The bullshitter may not deceive us, or even intend to do so, either about the facts or about what he takes the facts to be. What he does necessarily attempt to deceive us about is his enterprise. His only indispensably distinctive char-acteristic is that in a certain way he misrepresents what he is up to" (Frankfurt 2005, 54). So what the bullshitter conceals is not a lie but "that the truth-values of his statements are of no central interest to him" (55). And if the ruse of bullshit is ever detected, Frankfurt writes, audiences "are more likely to turn away from [bullshit] with an impatient or irritated shrug than with the sense of violation or outrage that lies often inspire" (50). This may help explain why Trump's bullshit was better received by the national audience than Hillary Clinton's lies. For audiences, I suppose, it is better to be the recipient of bullshit ("got me again") than to be the victim of a lie ("lock her up").

All of this is very interesting, but, as I have said, Frankfurt (and even Fredal) wrote their interpretations of bullshit before Brexit or the rise of Trump on the national political scene. They wrote, in other words, *pre-post-truth*. Now we can ask with the benefit of hindsight, "Has the status of bullshit changed post-truth?" The answer is, "Yes." As Justin E. H. Smith (2016) points out, with the rise of Trump as a politi-cian, "we see a disregard for truth that quite plainly cannot be understood in terms of bullshit. This is not the deviation from truth that we expect from a grafter or a con man, nor is it the pathological indifference to truth we expect from a loud-mouthed boaster. It is rather the audacious rejection of truth as a standard by which we all must be judged" (B4). I ague that this rejection is not just true of Trump but also true of the audiences he addresses.

One thing that has not changed in post-truth bullshit is the lack of any relationship to facts, realities, and truths among political rhetors and their rhetorical performances. However, both Frankfurt and Fredal exhibit a pre-post-truth mindset regarding audiences. They believe that audiences are either weak and thus susceptible to bullshit, or they are strong and will detect and discredit bullshit. These pre-post-truth audiences, then, still have a deep connection (or an unfortunate intellectual inability to connect) to facts, realities, and truths. Bullshit succeeds only if it, first, convinces audiences to accept bullshit as if it were truth and, second, manipulates audiences to misunderstand the motivation of the speaker. This is where pre-post-truth bullshit differs from post-truth bullshit. In post-truth bullshit, even the audiences have no concern for facts, realities, or truths, thus relieving speakers from the need to conceal their manipulative intent. Post-truth audiences accept bullshit as the norm in public discourse without objection because post-truth audiences, like bullshit rhetors, are now disassociated from the epistemological continuum. When politicians toe the party line in every instance, sometimes speaking absurdities in order to be ideologically consistent, audiences, toeing the same party line, accept these absurdities as facts of rhetorical life. In a post-truth world, audiences do not seek information on which to base their opinions; they seek opinions that support their own beliefs. In a world where facts, realities, and truths are irrelevant, language becomes pure strategy without grounding or reference. This is the central problem that post-truth rhetoric now poses for writing teachers. Bullshit was relatively simple in a pre-post-truth world, yet it has evolved, post-truth, into a complex array of related rhetorical strategies, including, for example, fake news.

Fake News

Before the post-truth world became so visible to journalists and critics in 2015 and 2016, big-money corporations (such as the tobacco industry and fossil fuel manufacturers) challenged fact-based policy making by overturning established and credible science with bogus research (Rabin-Havt 2016). Bogus research, funded by corporate money, is not intended to reveal the truth or even to lie; its intent is to sow seeds of doubt in the minds of policy makers and voting citizens, resulting in the status quo. Tobacco corporations, for example, have spent tens of millions of dollars funding research that challenges the addictive power of nicotine and the correlation of smoking with lung cancer. Fossil fuel manufacturers have spent tens of millions of dollars funding research that attributes climate change to natural causes, not human activities or carbon emissions. The result of this research is inaction in Congress, and thus no new regulations on industries that are clearly harming people and damaging the environment. In effect, Ari Rabin-Havt (2016) explains in *Lies, Incorporated*, "our democracy has been hacked, manipulated by political practitioners who recognize that as long as there is no truth, there can be no progress" (4). Bogus research is an effective means to manipulate public policy making, and I'm sure it still goes on post-truth, but this strategy has also evolved into other strategic means that take advantage of new social media platforms for quick dissemination. Bogus research is expensive and can be countered by real research, but post-truth fake news is significantly more slippery and probably more effective.

Pre-post-truth fake news has been around for quite a while. After the horrors of World War II, composition teachers were deeply concerned with the power and effect of Communist political propaganda on citizens in the United States, and they developed pedagogical strategies to combat this effect. *The Onion*, *The Daily Show*, and *The Colbert Report* have satirized news media for years, offering fake news as humor and entertainment. But post-truth "fake news" is something different.

In the fall of 2016, I got a text from my daughter while she was at school. I don't have it in my phone any more, but I remember it said something like, "Clowns terrorizing students at local schools today. Oak mtn on lockdown. Plz be here right when school lets out." I laughed, of course (clowns? really?), but my daughter was genuinely scared, so I, and about 900 other parents, got to the school early that day. There were security guards and local police everywhere. After we got home, I asked my daughter how she found out clowns were terrorizing students at local schools. She said that her friends saw it on Instagram. Apparently, these evil clowns, based in Georgia, have their own Instagram page, and some students found out from this source that the Birmingham suburbs were their next target.

Most of the adults involved thought this was just a ridiculous hoax, though area schools had no choice but to take the threat seriously. However, over the next few days news started to trickle in from reputable sources that clowns were being caught near local schools and arrested on charges of terrorism. (It is apparently not difficult to identify and arrest criminals wearing clown costumes.) Plainclothes police officers lurked in costume shops, surveilling anyone who bought clown attire. After a week or so, nine arrests of suspicious clowns (some carrying actual weapons) had been made across north-central Alabama. The notion that clowns with a real intent to do harm would advertise that fact on Instagram just seemed too silly to be true. But when the arrests started, no one knew what to think anymore. It was never clear to me whether or not the clowns who advertised their threat on Instagram ever made it to the Birmingham suburbs, so the clowns who had been arrested must have been of local origin. They joined in on the hoax after hearing about it online.

In this case of the terrorist clowns, the lines between true and false, real and fake, rumor and threat are hopelessly blurred. The original Instagram threat was most likely a hoax. But the fact is that this internet hoax incited actual criminal activity. Was it fake? Was it news? Yes, it was. Both. And this is why fake news is so troubling to people who care about reasoned arguments and facts as grounding for action and why it is so useful to people who use fake news in order to incite actions that the truth might otherwise discourage. Rob Boston (2016) points out that "in post-truth America, even implausible tales gain currency because some irresponsible politicians, eager for votes and cash, spread them. What's disturbing is the fact that these claims' implausibility doesn't slow them down. In fact, despite their implausibility, they are accepted by some who are then spurred to action—in some cases, violent action" (32).

Another recent example of fake news is called "pizza-gate." In the introduction to her story on the pizzagate event, Petula Dvorak (2016) writes: "The fake news stuff we've been talking about? That all just got real" (B2). On December 4, 2016, according to Luke O'Neil (2016), "a man was arrested after walking into a D.C. restaurant and firing at least one shot from an AR-15 rifle. Such an incident would not normally be considered national news in our trigger-happy culture, but the apparent motivation for this particular crime stands out. Edgar Welch, a 28-year-old from North Carolina, reportedly told police that he had come to the Comet Ping Pong pizza shop to self-investigate 'Pizzagate,' an exceedingly dumb right-wing hoax even graded on the forgiving curve for right-wing hoaxes."

O'Neil explains, "The theory, so crazy that even Reddit banned the page discussing it, goes as such: Hillary Clinton and John Podesta are at the center of a vast child-trafficking scheme with a pedophilia rape dungeon that just so happens to be located in the basement of an innocuous D.C. pizza shop."

This is *crazy*. Of course Clinton and Podesta aren't involved in a child-trafficking ring. It used to be that when people saw a story about George W. Bush's alien love child, they would understand, okay, that's a grocery store tabloid, so it's not real. But Dvorak (2016) writes, "[I]n today's social-media universe, there's a flood of stories from fake news sites that look legit," so much so that we share them freely on social media with others who also think they look legit (B2). Besides, regardless of how slick and official these sources may look, Cathleen Decker and Michael A. Memoli (2016) explain that traditional news sources "are no longer trusted and the vacuum has been filled by those spreading falsehoods" (A5).

The most common sources of fake news are websites (Real News Right Now, The Blaze, Ending the Fed, The Political Insider, and Breitbart, just to name a few, and more emerge every day) that generate untrue stories in order to create or reinforce strategic, advantageous beliefs (political, social) and make money. While bogus research costs millions each year, fake-news websites actually generate funds through advertising (Paresh 2016, C1). Further complicating matters, the more outrageous the stories published on the websites, the more viewer clicks they generate; the more viewer clicks the websites generate, the more money the sites' owners earn from companies whose products appear in banners and pop-ups. Since fake news receives more viewer interest (measured in "clicks") than real news, the financial motivation to publish fake news is greater than the financial motivation to publish real news.

In "The Story a News Faker Never Imagined," Caitlin Dewey (2016) prints an interview with Paul Horner, a "38-year-old impresario of a Facebook fake-news empire," who has successfully "made his living off viral news hoaxes for several years" (C1). In this interview, Horner says:

> Honestly, people [now] are definitely dumber. They just keep passing stuff around. Nobody fact-checks anything anymore—I mean, that's how Trump got elected. He just said whatever he wanted, and people believed everything, and when the things he said turned out not to be true, people didn't care because they'd already accepted it. It's real scary. I've never seen anything like it. . . . My [fake-news] sites were picked up by Trump supporters all the time. I think Trump is in the White House because of me. His followers don't fact-check anything—they'll post everything, believe anything. His campaign manager posted my story about a protester getting paid $3,500 as fact. Like, I made that up. . . . I thought they'd fact-check it, and it'd make them look worse. I mean, that's how this always works: Someone posts something I write, then they find out it's false, then they look like idiots. But Trump supporters—they just kept running with it! They never fact-check anything! Now he's in the White House. Looking back, instead of hurting the campaign, I think I helped it. (C1)

When Dewey asked Horner about the crackdown on fake news by its primary purveyors, Facebook and Google, Horner admitted he was nervous, since he currently makes $10,000 a month through ads on his fake-news websites. But, when Horner thinks about the whole issue less selfishly, he agrees: "There are so many horrible sites out there. I'm glad they're getting rid of those sites" (C1).

Fake-news writers compose outrageous stories either to make money from advertising or to attribute shameful qualities to certain people, usually political opponents (though, in the case of Trump and his campaign, social and cultural groups are also targets). These post-truth stories are then posted, tweeted, and tagged (etc.) on social media platforms without any context for criticism or judgment. As Amelia Tate (2016) explains, machines and algorithms cannot detect fake news, so social media sites like Facebook remain popular and safe venues for the spread of untrue stories. "The result," Cara Lombardo (2016) explains, "is an eerie uniformity among rightwing media and candidates, even on matters where they're objectively wrong. This dangerous duo implants phony memes into the national dialect and ricochets falsehoods around the world before the truth can get its shoes on" (20).

Lombardo (2016) argues that fact-checking websites like PolitiFact.com and FactCheck.org are helpful, but "by the time an analysis is published, sometimes just a day later, the statement in question will already have been echoed across the country. Those who already heard it are unlikely to revise their initial impressions, which makes false information a serious threat" (21). So serious, in fact, that fake news may have contributed to Trump's win in the 2016 US presidential election. Dana Milbank (2016) explains that an analysis published by the website BuzzFeed "concluded that fake news stories about the election generated more engagement on Facebook than the top election stories from 19 major news outlets—combined. And that's not the half of it. Not only is fake news getting more attention than actual news, but also the leading purveyor of fake news in the United States" is now the president (A17).

Mr. Trump is not the origin of the fake-news problem, but, as a *The Washington Post* editorial titled "Fake News, Real Gunfire" (2016) explains, he is certainly not a solution either, and he may be responsible for making fake news acceptable to a post-truth public: "Mr. Trump's embrace of conspiracy theories created a safe-zone for fact-free discourse. His birther obsession; his hint that Justice Antonin Scalia may have been murdered; his assertions that Muslims in New Jersey cheered as they watched the Sept. 11 attacks; his comments associating Sen. Ted Cruz's father with President Kennedy's assassination—all of that has normalized the bogus and dissolved the opprobrium that traditionally attached to public figures who traded in falsehoods" (A18). So what of the future? When will the fake-news empire crumble under the weight of its own absurdity? *New York Times* columnist Nicholas Kristof (2016) is not hopeful: "The landscape ahead looks grim to me. While the business model for mainstream journalism is in crisis, the alt-right websites expand as they monetize false 'news' that promotes racism and undermines democracy. Worse, they have the imprimatur of the soon-to-be most powerful person in the world" (SR11).

Fake news is an insidious form of post-truth rhetoric, and social media exponentially increases the problems of misinformation and narrow-mindedness. For an ever-growing number of people who get their information online, social media platforms both feed content that viewers already agree with and encourage ideological social grouping, limiting encounters with different ideas that may challenge settled beliefs. In "Yes, I'd Lie to You" (2016), the author explains, "The tendency of netizens to form self-contained groups is strengthened by what Eli Pariser, an internet activist, identified five years ago as the 'filter bubble.' Back in 2011, he worried that Google's search algorithms, which offer users personalized results according to what the system knows of their preferences and surfing behaviors, would keep people from coming across contravailing views" (also see Viner 2016). For example, Facebook's "algorithms are designed to populate [users'] news feeds with content similar to material previously 'liked'" ("Yes, I'd Lie to You" 2016). Katharine Murphy (2016) explains:

"There is a massive appetite for gut validation. Increasingly, audiences want to choose their own facts, and read opinions they agree with. The trend is reinforced by social media algorithms which push agreeable content in the direction of the consumer, and screen out irritations such as alternative points of view."

While social media platforms like Twitter and Facebook and search engines like Google defend their use of algorithms that generate customized content, the fact is that this sort of approach to online content contradicts the original purpose of the internet. Katharine Viner (2016) writes: "Publications curated by editors have in many cases been replaced by a stream of information chosen by friends, contacts, and family, processed by secret algorithms. The old idea of a wide-open web—where hyperlinks from site to site created a non-hierarchical and decentralized network of information—has been largely supplanted by platforms designed to maximize your time within their walls, some of which (such as Instagram and Snapchat) do not allow outward links at all." So online rumor-mongering and the isolationism and insularity resulting from the algorithms behind social media platforms have amplified the problem of fake news exponentially. Fake news is insidious post-truth rhetoric with very real consequences.

Ethos (at the Expense of Logos)

Rhetorics, ancient and modern, have always valued logos in addition to ethos and pathos (though if one is denigrated, it is usually pathos). Logos is what moves arguments along their paths from premises to conclusions, and ethos and pathos supplement this movement, making it more persuasive. But in the topsy-turvy world of post-truth rhetoric, ethos and pathos have themselves become effective sources of arguments, and logos is actually denigrated.

Trump has a big personality, larger than life, but personality is not the same thing as ethos or credibility. Personality can be described in psychological terms as this or that; it is the sum of individual qualities, usually resulting from a series of unique life-experiences. Ethos is inherently relational, like most rhetorical concepts. It describes the rhetorical effect (in terms of credibility) that one personality has on another personality's willingness or capacity to be persuaded. Yet personality is also the beginning point of any study of a rhetor's ethos.

In "The Mind of Donald Trump," Donald P. McAdams (2016), a professor of psychology at Northwestern University, examines Trump's written and spoken discourses in order to characterize his personality and predict what sort of president he might make. This essay was published in *The Atlantic* magazine five months before the election, but McAdams takes seriously the possibility that Trump might actually win. Good thing. Trump won. Although McAdams isolates extreme narcissism, disagreeableness, and grandiosity as some of Trump's most dominant personality traits, what strikes me as the most relevant characteristic in terms of Trump's post-truth rhetoric is that he always seems to be acting. McAdams writes, "More than even Ronald Reagan, Trump seems supremely cognizant of the fact that he is always acting. He moves through life like a man who knows he is always being observed. If all human beings are, by their very nature, social actors, then Donald Trump seems to be more so—superhuman, in this one primal sense" (78). If ethos is relational, and credibility derives from an audience's response to the personality of a speaker, what happens to ethos when the speaker is always acting, always putting on whatever personality traits might be effective in any given rhetorical situation? Like the language of bullshit and fake news, post-truth ethos becomes purely strategic, unencumbered by the reasoning of logos. Post-truth ethos is the performance of credibility, whether that credibility is real or fake.

McAdams characterizes Trump's personality by plotting his actions and words across psychology's "Big Five" high-low continua of personality characteristics: extroversion, neuroticism, conscientiousness, agreeableness, and openness. According to McAdams, "Across his lifetime, Donald Trump has exhibited a trait profile that you would not expect of a U.S. president: sky-high extroversion combined with off-the-chart low agreeableness" (79). Although Trump is mostly a disagreeable person, he "plays his role in an outgoing, exuberant, and socially dominant manner" (79), attracting interest from people who mistake his narcissistic extroversion for confidence and his neurotic disagreeableness for honesty. Trump's extroversion correlates to "relentless reward-seeking," especially "in the form of social approval, fame, or wealth" (79). Trump's constant refrain on the campaign trail is characteristic of his need for victory: "Oh, we're gonna win. We're gonna win. We're gonna win so big. So big."

It is no accident that Aristotle, in response to certain Greek sophists, and Quintilian, in response to the Roman emperors, both eliminated any notion of success from their definitions of rhetoric. Trump, like Aristotle's sophists and Quintilian's emperors, cares little about *perceiving* in any given case the available means of persuasion, and he cares even less about the inherent goodness of the rhetor. Trump will use any rhetorical strategy to win, even if it violates every ethical principle associated with the art of rhetoric; and he will project any personal qualities that get the job done, even if they are not good. Using post-truth ethos (at the expense of logos), Trump projects not his personality traits for others to judge but whatever personality traits will win the rhetorical day. Trump is a first-rate actor in his post-truth world of made-up credibility.

Although, as McAdams (2016) points out, "Research shows that people low in agreeableness are typically viewed as untrustworthy" (81), Trump seems to actually benefit from this trait. Establishment politicians campaign on the promise of trustworthiness, but in Trump's topsy-turvy post-truth rhetorical world, the audiences that have gravitated toward Trump value his ability to make a deal by any means necessary. Establishment politicians have said they were trustworthy, but then they weren't. Trump makes no claims toward trustworthiness, so that's better, the thinking goes. In a post-truth rhetorical world, blatant untrustworthiness, as a personality trait, may be more valuable than feigned trustworthiness, as establishment politicians have exhibited for the past several decades. With the disaffected voters in the US, it's better to know what you're getting than to think you're getting one thing and then get something else.

Trump's untrustworthiness, and his audience's acceptance of it, extends from his more general "authoritarian personality" (McAdams 2016, 82), which, for many citizens living in a free democracy, is Trump's most troubling trait, but it is also the trait that is most attractive to citizens who have long felt disenfranchised by the democratic process. McAdams writes, "Among white Americans, high scores on measures of authoritarianism today tend to be associated with prejudice against a wide range of 'out-groups,' including homosexuals, African Americans, immigrants, and Muslims. Authoritarianism is also associated with suspiciousness of the humanities and the arts, and with cognitive rigidity, militaristic sentiments, and Christian fundamentalism" (82). However, McAdams continues: "When individuals with authoritarian proclivities fear that their way of life is being threatened, they may turn to strong leaders who promise to keep them safe—leaders like Donald

Trump. In a national poll conducted recently by the political scientist Matthew MacWilliams, high levels of authoritarianism emerged as the single strongest predictor of expressing political support for Donald Trump" (82).

In the end, Trump's ethos (because ethos is relational) emerges only when audiences respond to Trump's personality, so a single politician may have multiple manifestations of ethos depending on the personality of the audience. Many people believe Trump's bullshit because of the power of his ethos, yet his ethos is also what turns off so many people. In fact, Smith (2016) writes: "Much of the disagreement about Donald Trump among American voters has to do with which sort of character he is: a lowly fraudster or a larger-than-life revaluer of values. It does not have to do with whether or not he is telling the truth. And so, frustratingly to many opponents, simply pointing out that he is speaking falsehoods can do nothing to set him back" (B4).

In a post-truth world, even the ethos of what used to count as institutions promoting truth and critical thinking has been challenged. In "Yes, I'd Lie to You" (2016), the author explains, "[M]any societies have developed institutions which allow some consensus over what truth is: schools, science, the legal system, the media." However, in some places, "this truth-producing infrastructure" has "been systematically undermined." In other words, the very credibility of knowledge-producing institutions has been called into questions, leaving spin doctors and talking heads to tell us what to believe. Ruth Marcus (2016) agrees, suggesting, "In this post-truth universe, institutions—news media, the intelligence community—are drained of all credibility. . . . With facts passé, the next, inexorable move is to reduce all news to the same level of distrust and disbelief. . . . Journalism is an inherently imperfect profession. We write the first rough draft of history—as best we can, subject to correction and revision. But there is a difference between inevitably flawed and intentionally false. To deliberately blur this distinction is to seek to undermine the central role of media in a free society" (A17). Yet in Trump's post-truth world, undermining the ethos of the media is exactly the goal. Marcus explains that Trump's rhetorical goal is "a society in which all truth is malleable and all news is suspect. Whose voice, whose vision, whose authority will then be trusted? Trump doesn't say, but it is not hard to guess" (A17).

When Trump is challenged on his bullshit, his rebuttals do not attempt to establish or reinforce the truth-value of his claims since his bullshit ethos requires no attachment to reasoning. Instead, when Trump is challenged, he attacks the credibility of the knowledge-producing institutions that are responsible for the challenge. Jeet Heer (2015) describes two examples of Trump's bullshit/challenge/rebuttal process that are especially instructive. These examples demonstrate why "Trump is so unfazed when called on his bullshit. Trump's frequent response is to undermine the very possibility that the truth of his claims are knowable."

In Heer's (2015) first example, Trump makes a claim about the Muslim response to the 9/11 terrorist attacks, and then he calls into question the media's capacity to know the truth of anything that happened more than two years ago because of changes in media technologies:

> Among the recent Trumpian untruths is his claim to have seen a video showing "thousands and thousands" of Muslim Americans cheering 9/11 in Jersey City, New Jersey, an event there is no record of, video or otherwise. ∴ .
>
> When asked why there are no videos of "thousands and thousands" of Muslim-Americans cheering the 9/11 attacks,

Trump told Joe Scarborough that 2001 was so far in the past that the evidence has disappeared. "Don't forget, 14, 15 years ago, it wasn't like it is today, where you press a button and you play a video," Trump said in a phone interview on yesterday's *Morning Joe*. "Fourteen, 15 years ago, they don't even put it in files, they destroy half of the stuff. You know, if you look back 14, 15 years, that was like ancient times in terms of cinema, and in terms of news and everything else. They don't have the same stuff. Today you can press a button and you can see exactly what went on, you know, two years ago. But when you go back 14, 15 years, that's like ancient technology, Joe."

This claim—that he's telling the truth but that there can be no proof of it—is in some ways more insidious than the initial falsehood. It takes us to a post-truth world where Trump's statements can't be fact-checked, and we have to simply accept the workings of his self-proclaimed "world's greatest memory." In effect, Trump wants to take us to a land where subjectivity is all, where reality is simply what he says.

In Heer's (2015) second example, Trump is challenged about the historical veracity of a Civil War memorial plaque displayed at a Trump-owned golf course. Trump's rebuttal does not attempt to establish the veracity of the plaque's historical claim but instead attacks the credibility of academic historians to know anything they did not witness personally. Heer writes:

> A similar gambit to destroy the possibility of objective historical knowledge can be seén in a controversy over a Civil War memorial plaque at a Trump golf course in Sterling, Virginia. The plaque reads: "Many great American soldiers, both of the North and South, died at this spot. The casualties were so great that the water would turn red and thus became known as 'The River of Blood.'" When informed by *The New York Times* that historians called the plaque a fiction because there is no record of a battle fought on that spot, Trump petulantly responded: "How would they know that? . . . Were they there?" Again, what's disturbing here is an attack on the hard-won scholarship

that tries to sift through the evidence of the past to accurately record history. In Trump's bullshit universe, history is whatever is convenient for him to say.

In these two examples, it is clear that Trump's own credibility is at rhetorical war with the credibility of the news media and of academic historians. Whenever Trump's own ethos is challenged as lacking any foundation in logos (lacking, that is, any reasoning or evidence for his claims), Trump's post-truth response is not to then back his claims with logos but to challenge the attacker's ethos as lacking logos (i.e., lacking evidence that Trump's claims are false).

Pathos (at the Expense of Logos)

Pathos occupies an important function in post-truth rhetoric. Bullshit and fake news, regardless of truth-value or reasoning, reinforce and intensify current beliefs, so if rhetors can control those current beliefs through emotional appeals (prior to the strategic use of bullshit and fake news), then the persuasive effect of bullshit and fake news is also reinforced and intensified. In other words, if rhetors can control the emotional foundations of their audiences' beliefs, then they can feed their audiences any line of bullshit or fake news whatsoever, and these audiences will accept it without question. Viner (2016) writes, "When a fact begins to resemble whatever you feel is true, it becomes very difficult for anyone to tell the difference between facts that are true 'and 'facts' that are not." Trump, for example, has whipped up anger in a larger-than-expected alt-right audience, making their rage fertile soil in which to plant seeds of opposition and giving voice to a previously disaffected fringe. This anger that Trump taps into makes it easy for him and his staff to spread bullshit and fake news that alt-right audiences soak in and even, unfortunately, act upon. Trump's bullshit and fake news are false and completely made up. However, the anger that was latent in Trump's audience and then made manifest through his own angry rhetoric not only has resulted in an unwillingness by Trump's audience to fact-check crazy statements and fake stories but has also led them to circulate these statements and stories exponentially through social media, retweeting them on Twitter and reposting them on Facebook (etc.) until bullshit statements and fake-news stories outnumber credible news articles twenty-to-one.

According to McAdams (2016), this anger that Trump whips up in his alt-right audience lies at the core of his own personality. The emotions that emerge from Trump's personality, such as anger, resonate with a certain ultra-conservative audience in the US. McAdams writes, "Arguably the most highly valued human trait the world over, agreeableness pertains to the extent to which a person appears to be caring, loving, affectionate, polite, and kind" (79). Trump, however, is "a remarkably disagreeable person" (80), with *anger* at his "emotional core" (80). Aristotle talks about anger as a rhetorical strategy to counter apathy in audiences, for example. But McAdams argues that anger is "the operative emotion" behind Trump's personality, not just an emotional source of arguments for constructing enthymemes and persuading audiences. According to McAdams, "anger lies at the heart of Trump's charisma. And anger permeates his political rhetoric" (80). Since Trump is "markedly less ideological than most presidential candidates" (81), the anger that characterizes his emotional state may become a significantly prominent aspect of his decision-making process.

In addition to building up his own credibility (at least with certain kinds of citizens) and destroying the credibility of people and institutions that challenge him, it has been clear throughout the campaign and election process that Trump's goal is to persuade disaffected citizens to vote for him not through reasoned argumentation but through whipping up their emotions ("What the hell do you have to lose?"). In "Yes, I'd Lie to You" (2016), the author explains: "There is a strong case that, in America and elsewhere, there is a shift towards a politics in which feelings trump facts more freely and with less resistance than used to be the case. . . . The post-truth strategy works because it allows people to forgo critical thinking in favor of having their feelings reinforced by soundbite truthiness." Marcus (2016) agrees, suggesting that "[e]motion outranks fact; believing makes it so. We are all Tinkerbell now. Clap if you believe in voter fraud. Clap if you doubt a human role in climate change" (A17).

On June 16, 2015, Trump gave a speech in front of Trump Tower in New York City announcing his candidacy for the 2016 presidential election. This speech is the first major public event Trump used to establish a base of support, create an audience receptive to his rhetoric, and define the terms of his campaign.[8] It is filled with emotional appeals to a disaffected alt-right community, and it is driven by the anger that forms the core of Trump's personality. Throughout the speech, Trump uses at least three rhetorical strategies that emphasize pathos as a means of persuasion: name-calling, hyperbole, and metaphor.

The most infamous name-calling example in Trump's election-bid announcement speech is when he calls Mexicans in the US drug dealers, criminals, and rapists, hoping to elicit nationalistic anger and anxiety over immigration. Trump says: "When Mexico sends its people, they're not sending their best. They're not sending you. They're not sending you. They're sending people that have lots of problems, and they're bringing those problems with us. They're bringing drugs. They're bringing crime. They're rapists. And some, I assume, are good people." For an

alt-right audience that is already concerned about the relationship between crime and immigration (because they believe
political bullshit and fake news), this statement taps into and
also intensifies existing fears. Despite the statement's overt racism, Trump succeeds in solidifying support among xenophobes
through appeals to pathos that have no basis in truth or reality
or reasoning.

As the speech progresses, Trump calls politicians in
Washington, DC, stupid and losers, highlighting his anti-poli-
tician and anti-establishment stance in the race. He says: "Right
now, think of this: We owe China $1.3 trillion. We owe Japan
more than that. So they come in, they take our jobs, they take
our money, and then they loan us back the money, and we pay
them in interest, and then the dollar goes up so their deal's even
better. How stupid are our leaders? How stupid are these politicians to allow this to happen? How stupid are they?" Later,
Trump says: "We have losers. We have losers. We have people
that don't have it. We have people that are morally corrupt. We
have people that are selling this country down the drain." The
words *stupid* and *loser* are hurtful, and they are bullshit when
applied to politicians who have genuine policy disagreements.
The words *stupid* and *loser* make Trump's audience members
feel that they and Trump are better and smarter than our established government officials, so replacing them with Trump at
the helm is the only reasonable course of action.

There are lots of other examples of name calling in this
speech, but these few illustrate well enough that Trump uses
name-calling as a rhetorical strategy based in pathos in order
to elicit anger and anxiety over immigration and trade. Since
Trump's alt-right audience already holds these sentiments, he
uses pathetic name-calling as a way to reinforce and intensify
the anger and anxiety that his audience already feels.

Name-calling is a form of hyperbole, of course: it is an exaggeration to say that Mexicans in America are mostly rapists and drug dealers, and not all politicians are stupid losers. But there are (plenty of) other examples in which Trump deliberately exaggerates information in order to elicit fear over trade and unemployment. Trump says: "When do we beat Mexico at the border? They're laughing at us, at our stupidity. And now they are beating us economically. They are not our friend, believe me. But they're killing us economically." It is obviously an exaggeration to say that Mexicans are laughing at us and are killing us, but for an audience that already harbors nationalistic resentment at Democratic openness toward immigration, these exaggerations sound about right.

Later in the speech, Trump exaggerates statistics about the US gross domestic product (GDP) and unemployment rates. Trump says: "Last quarter it was just announced our gross domestic product—a sign of strength, right? But not for us. It was below zero. Whoever heard of this? It's never below zero. Our labor participation rate was the worst since 1978. But think of it, GDP below zero, horrible labor participation rate. And our real unemployment is anywhere from 18 to 20 percent. Don't believe the 5.6. Don't believe it. That's right. A lot of people up there can't get jobs. They can't get jobs, because there are no jobs, because China has our jobs and Mexico has our jobs. They all have jobs. But the real number, the real number is anywhere from 18 to 19 and maybe even 21 percent, and nobody talks about it, because it's a statistic that's full of nonsense." The numbers that Trump provides are exaggerations (if not lies, though we are talking post-truth now, so . . .).

No source that I have founds lists the US GDP at the time of this speech as zero. But "zero" is a powerful word that elicits deep emotions for people who believe the economy did not improve in the eight years of Obama's presidency. And unemployment rates may have been in the teens in certain areas of certain cities at the time of the speech, but Trump cites these numbers as if they represent a national average. I cannot find a single source that lists national unemployment anywhere close to Trump's numbers. But for an audience that is already concerned about the economy (despite objective measures that point only to improvement), these figures (zero GDP and 21 percent unemployment) reinforce anger that already exists.

Trump also uses metaphors as a way to relate political matters to the everyday lives of his audiences, also eliciting advantageous emotions in them. On trade, for example, Trump invokes military metaphors, relating our economic relationship with China to a war: "Our country is in serious trouble. We don't have victories anymore. We used to have victories, but we don't have them. When was the last time anybody saw us beating, let's say, China in a trade deal? They kill us. I beat China all the time. All the time. . . . I own a big chunk of the Bank of America building at 1290 Avenue of the Americas, that I got from China in a war. Very valuable." Also regarding China's trade practices with the US, Trump uses a sports metaphor to show the discrepancy between Chinese negotiators and US negotiators: "No, I love [China]. But their leaders are much smarter than our leaders, and we can't sustain [ourselves] with that. There's too much—it's like—it's like take the New England Patriots and Tom Brady and have them play your high school football team. That's the difference between China's leaders and our leaders." Finally, Trump uses biblical imagery to intensify how effective he will be as president: "[Politicians] will not bring us—believe me—to the promised land. They will not. . . . I will be the greatest jobs president that God ever created. I tell you that."

In these metaphorical passages, Trump compares trade negotiations with China to a war and a football game, and he compares himself to Moses and fancies himself one of God's greatest creations. Most of Trump's alt-right audiences may relate to war and football more easily than they may relate to trade negotiations with China, so that connection makes Trump's bullshit argument hit closer to home than a bland economic argument might. And Trump's alt-right audiences may view him as the political savior they have been waiting for, sent by God, and Trump seems perfectly willing to invoke that role for himself.

Trump uses other means to elicit emotional responses in his audiences, but in this speech, name-calling, hyperbole, and metaphor seem to be the most prominent and most effective. In his later speeches and debates, these strategies and others take center stage in Trump's rhetoric. But this speech, announcing his bid for the Republican nomination, set a pathetic rhetorical tone that would continue for at least another year.

The Trump Effect

Although the term "Trump effect" has been defined in different ways, I prefer to think of it as the material and social results of successful post-truth rhetoric. Throughout the 2016 campaign for president of the United States, post-truth rhetoric was employed primarily (though not exclusively) by one candidate, Trump, and his campaign staff. Post-truth rhetoric, as I have said, is based on bullshit parading as truth, xenophobia parading as patriotism, and ethos and pathos parading as logos, among other things; the effects of all of this post-truth rhetoric—the Trump effect—are anger, fear, angst, and violence. A Briefing article in *The Economist* (2016) explains, "Mr. Trump appears not to care whether his words bear any relation to reality, so long as they fire up voters" ("Yes, I'd Lie to You" 2016). During the campaign, and especially since the November 8, 2016, election, the media have been excoriating Trump for his bullshit, but the Trump effect is also very much a function of media practices. Brogan Morris (2016) writes, "The media helped to create Donald Trump by insisting that whatever he said, no matter how outrageous, was worth airing, thus giving import to his nonsense."

Throughout the 2016 campaign, the Southern Poverty Law Center (SPLC), a liberal organization devoted to social justice, published a series of three articles detailing the Trump effect, or the effect of Trump's post-truth rhetoric, particularly on schools across the country. In "The Trump Effect: The Impact of the Presidential Campaign on Our Nation's Schools," published on their website on April 13, 2016, the SPLC writes, "[T]he campaign is producing an alarming level of fear and anxiety among children of color and inflaming racial and ethnic tensions in the classroom" (under "Introduction"). The SPLC reports, "Teachers have noted an increase in bullying, harassment, and intimidation of students whose races, religions, or nationalities have been the verbal targets of candidates on the campaign trail," while other students from cultural and racial majorities "have been emboldened by the divisive, often juvenile rhetoric in the campaign" (under "Introduction"). Here are just a few examples of the kinds of divisive and xenophobic arguments that the SPLC isolates as having a "profoundly negative effect" on children and schools: "During the campaign, Trump has spoken of deporting millions of Latino immigrants, building a wall between the United States and Mexico, banning Muslim immigrants, and even killing the families of Islamist terrorists. He has also called Mexican immigrants 'rapists' and drug dealers" (under "Introduction"). While it is true that we are living in a new world of post-truth rhetoric, the fact is that Trump has been its primary purveyor during the past year, so much so that his name is used as a racial and cultural slur: "some are using the word Trump as a taunt or as a chant as they gang up on others" (under "Introduction"). This kind of taunting has become the norm in public discourse across the country, but especially in our nation's schools. According to the SPLC, "Teachers report an increase in anger and 'acting out' among students and a decreased ability to engage in civil discourse. Discussions turn into shouting matches, verbal hostility, and sometimes even fights" (under "Behavior Is Harder to Manage and Explain").

The second article in the SPLC series, "The Trump Effect: The Impact of the 2016 Presidential Election on Our Nation's Schools," reports results of a survey administered in the first few days after the November 8 election, though it was not published on the website until November 28. This article, written by Maureen B. Costello (2016), explains that the situation discussed in the first article (above) has worsened. Costello writes, "Ninety percent of educators [who responded to the survey] report that school climate has been negatively affected, and most of them believe it will have a long-lasting impact" (under "Executive Summary"). Since April, Costello notes, a number of disturbing trends have been "on the upswing," including "verbal harassment, the use of slur and derogatory language, and disturbing incidents involving swastikas, Nazi salutes, and Confederate flags" (under "Executive Summary"). Costello and the SPLC directly attribute this degradation in public civil discourse to Trump and his election to the presidency of the United States. Costello writes, "Since Trump was elected, media have been awash in reports of hate incidents around the nation, including at schools." This "distinct uptick" in hate incidents "can be traced directly to the results of the election";

they "are nothing short of a crisis and should be treated as such" (under "Executive Summary"). For schools, this crisis is a drain on already underfunded resources: "The trauma students are experiencing is putting a strain on school counseling and social work resources and leading teachers to spend more time away from instruction so they can provide emotional support. . . . It's impossible to know how long added support will be needed and when trust will be restored" (under "The New Majority: Trauma and Fear"). Costello ends this report with some recommendations for teachers, including "set the tone"; "take care of the wounded"; "double-down on anti-bullying strategies"; "encourage courage"; and "be ready for a crisis" (under "Recommendations").

The third article published by the Southern Poverty Law Center, "Ten Days After: Harassment and Intimidation in the Aftermath of the Election," continues the grim story begun in the first two articles, with authors Cassie Miller and Alexandra Werner-Winslow (2016) describing "a national outbreak of hate, as white supremacists celebrate Donald Trump's victory" in the 2016 US presidential election (under "Introduction"). This rise of white supremacist language and action, the direct result of Trump's election, should come as no surprise to socially-minded rhetoricians (or anyone else, really): "Both the harassment since the election and the energy on the radical right [or white supremacist alt-right] are the predictable results of the campaign that Trump waged for the presidency—a campaign marked by incendiary racial statements, the stroking of white racial resentment, and attacks on so-called 'political correctness'" (under "Introduction"). Since the election, immigrant families have been the most affected by the negative campaign rhetoric. Miller and Werner-Winslow write: "Students and young people have absorbed divisive campaign rhetoric and are using it to taunt and harass their classmates, with chants of 'Build the wall!' making their way into school cafeterias, hallways, and buses" (under "Anti-Immigrant"). African Americans have suffered threats of lynching, many of which feature references to Trump (under "Anti-Black"). Negative campaign rhetoric has also resulted in hate incidents against Muslims, LGBT individuals, and women in general. Miller and Werner-Winslow point out that these hate incidents are grounded in anti-Semitism and white nationalism that was stirred up by the campaign rhetoric of Trump. Miller and Werner-Winslow hint at a solution to the problems they describe: "Rather than feign ignorance, [Trump] must acknowledge that his own words have opened 'wounds of division' in our country. Rather than simply saying 'Stop it!' and disavowing the radical right, he must speak out forcefully and repeatedly against all forms of bigotry and reach out to the communities his words have injured. And rather than merely saying that he 'wants to bring the country together,' his actions must consistently demonstrate he is doing everything in his power to do so. Until president-elect Trump does these things, the hate that his campaign has unleashed is likely to continue to flourish" (under "Introduction").

As Susan Miller-Cochran, Gregory Clark, and the CCCC leadership team have all indicated in their statements following the election (discussed above and quoted in the notes), it is painfully obvious that social justice and the rhetoric and writing that promote it are up to us. We cannot wait for Trump to do what is right.

POST-TRUTH COMPOSITION

In the introduction to this essay, I discussed three organizational responses to the 2016 presidential campaign and election (by

RSA, CWPA, and CCCC). These organizational responses, all sent to their members and published on their respective websites, deplore the current state of rhetorical practice in public discourse and call on their members to challenge post-truth rhetoric (though they do not directly use that term). The fact is, rhetoric and composition have had the tools to combat post-truth rhetoric for years, and we, as a community of scholars and teachers, need to double-down on those tools.

If post-truth rhetoric is left unchecked to infect public discourse even further, it will no doubt have a profoundly negative influence on composition studies. Post-truth rhetoric succeeds through bullshit, fake news, vicious social media posts, false denials, attacks on media, ethos and pathos at the expense of logos, and name-calling. These post-truth rhetorical strategies are anathema to every core value that writing teachers hold dear. However, I also believe that writing teachers have great potential to check and counter the negative influence of post-truth rhetoric in both composition classrooms and public discourse more generally. Writing teachers, perhaps better than anyone else, can prepare the next generation of voting citizens to recognize and fight against the kind of rhetoric that characterizes the current political climate, and we can teach students to use language that represents the values we already promote in our discipline, including those values described in the *Framework for Success in Postsecondary Writing* and the *WPA Outcomes Statement for First-Year Composition*.

The *Framework* (2011) describes eight habits of mind, or "ways of approaching learning that are both intellectual and practical" (4): curiosity, openness, engagement, creativity, persistence, responsibility, flexibility, and metacognition. Post-truth rhetoric requires for its success the inability in its audiences to engage in any of these habits of mind. Simply teaching writing as an exercise in developing the habits of mind described in the *Framework* will help to check and counter some of the effects of post-truth rhetoric on future audiences.

The success of bullshit, for example, requires audiences that are not curious: these audiences fear the outside world and do not want to know more about it; they seek and value only information that already supports their restricted belief systems. Teach curiosity, and you teach a potential counter to the susceptibility to bullshit.

The success of fake news requires audiences that are not open or engaged. Fake news succeeds because it is spread within the isolating context of social media filter bubbles, which prevent people from connecting with others who may have different beliefs. If students receive their news through Facebook, Google, Instagram, or Twitter, for example, then they see only news filtered through ideologically restrictive algorithms that present them with ideas they already believe, and so their beliefs are never challenged or expanded. Teach openness and engagement, and you teach potential counters to a destructive belief in fake news.

The success of appeals to ethos and pathos (at the expense of logos) requires audiences that are not persistent or responsible. Ethos and pathos succeed in the absence of reasoning only when audiences do not explore topics or ideas beyond taking someone's word for it or being moved emotionally by derogatory name-calling, misleading hyperboles, and distracting metaphors. Audiences that are susceptible to ethos and pathos do not consider the consequences of shallow beliefs and knee-jerk responses because they accept the opinions of those who reinforce their own ideas, and they allow their passions to bypass any appeal to reasoned opinion. Teach persistence and responsibility, and you teach potential counters to the rule of ethos and pathos at the expense of logos.

Teaching creativity, flexibility, and openness may help students understand and counter the Trump effect. The Trump effect exists because post-truth rhetoric has been normalized in public discourse by the language of the 2016 presidential campaign and election. If students can develop creative ways to communicate complex ideas, learn ways to adapt to new contexts, and reflect on how social institutions structure knowledge and emotions, then the Trump effect may lose strength. Unfortunately, the poster child of post-truth rhetoric is now our president, and the bullshit, fake news, and ethos and pathos are only intensifying. This reality makes our commitment to the habits of mind described in the *Framework* all the more critical. Teach students creativity, flexibility, and openness, and you teach students skills both to avoid using and to challenge others' use of the negative linguistic and social behaviors that are associated with the Trump effect.

Like the *Framework*, the *WPA Outcomes Statement* (2014) articulates values shared by writing teachers, and post-truth rhetoric cannot survive in the rhetorical environment described in the outcomes. The *Outcomes Statement* identifies four categories of conceptual knowledge and practical skills students should attain. By the end of their first-year writing experience, students should gain rhetorical knowledge; acquire skills in critical thinking, reading, and composing; understand the different processes of composing in different contexts and media; and develop a knowledge of conventions and their variability across genres. If students acquire the conceptual knowledge and practical skills described in the *Outcomes Statement*, the very foundations of post-truth rhetoric will begin to crumble.

When students develop skills in critical thinking, reading, and composing, they acquire the ability to identify, analyze, and critique bullshit. The success of bullshit is predicated on the absence of critical thinking, reading, and writing in its audiences, so simply teaching these rhetorical skills is one step in the direction of challenging the success of bullshit in public discourse. What critical thinking, reading, and writing can accomplish is the reassertion of truth and reality into the epistemological continuum, even if our own and our students' commitments are with reasoned opinions and sound arguments, not truth. Understanding that truth is on the epistemological continuum means that the old nemeses of truth (lies, fallacies, and doublespeak) also return to the continuum. Teaching students about the relationship between assertions and evidence results in the expectation that a claim alone, unsupported by backing or research, is insufficient to warrant belief.

Gaining rhetorical knowledge can help students challenge the manipulative effects of fake news. Students cannot consciously understand, analyze, or critique unethical rhetorical practices such as fake news without a grounding in the key concepts of rhetorical criticism. With this grounding, students can then explore and evaluate the different genres through which they acquire news. Given examples of fake news, such as "pizzagate," students can begin to understand the rhetorical qualities of the fake-news genre and how these qualities effect persuasion without any connection to truth or reality. Students can also begin to explore how the social media technologies that distribute fake news influence the ways in which readers process information in the context of filter bubbles.

Gaining knowledge of conventions and how they influence rhetorical processes can help students challenge the unethical effects of ethos and pathos at the expense of logos. When students see that rhetorical conventions vary from one genre to the next, they can begin to understand that certain genres, such as brief posts on social media sites, lack the kind of sound arguments that characterize reputable news outlets. Understanding these conventions helps students recognize why a tweet, for example, may be effective because the writer has credibility even though the argument itself is unsupported and may well be complete bullshit. And knowledge of conventions also shows students that certain genres, such as Facebook posts, are conducive to whipping up emotions in audiences but are not conducive to evidence-based argumentation.

Acquiring flexibility in their use of composing processes can help students contribute to a more ethical use of language, thereby combating the effects of post-truth rhetoric, the Trump effect. Learning to slow down and revise their arguments into complex statements of belief, rather than vague tweets and posts, helps students to see the structures of belief that ground potential action. And when students engage with other writers in the process of composing these complex statements, they encounter different beliefs and must engage with them in their own writing. Understanding that all beliefs and actions are both complex and social will help students understand that the Trump effect is based on simple ideas that cannot be supported in any significant way. When students collaborate on writing projects, they negotiate among the ideas of students in their writing groups, learning skills that can directly counter the Trump effect in the classroom and in public discourse.

While we all value the *Framework* and *Outcomes Statement* as texts that guide our profession, more than ever before we need to understand how these texts ground our discipline in ethical rhetorical practices and can be used to challenge the unethical rhetorical practices that have emerged post-truth. Also, writing teachers need to address post-truth rhetoric directly in their classrooms, offering for discussion, analysis, and critique a variety of examples of post-truth rhetoric, including bullshit (though we may call it something else), fake news, and texts that exploit ethos and pathos, and we need to address the Trump effect through the social dimensions of language. We must teach post-truth rhetoric as unethical language or it will infect our classrooms and public discourse irretrievably.

CONSEQUENCES OF NEGLECTING TO ACT

If I'm right that the effects of post-truth rhetoric may devastate composition studies if left unchecked, and that a plan for action already exists in disciplinary white papers like the *Framework for Success in Postsecondary Writing* and the *WPA Outcomes Statement for First-Year Composition*, then neglecting to act is inexcusable on our part. We need to double-down on the values we have already articulated and publicized. The consequences are too serious to let post-truth rhetoric go unchecked, and writing teachers are in a good position to fight against its effects.

If post-truth rhetoric goes unchecked, then the fears that were the exigence of the three organizational statements following the 2016 presidential campaign and election will become realities. Xenophobia will replace social justice, isolationism will invalidate cultural freedom, shouting will trump listening, disruption will drown out response, insults will replace respect, exclusion will diminish diversity, divisiveness will preclude negotiation, invective will erode support, fear will challenge safety, and success at all costs will invalidate responsible inquiry. This is not post-truth bullshit; this is the Trump effect, and it is already happening.

If we as a community, committed to social justice, cultural freedom, listening, response, respect, diversity, negotiation, support, and responsible inquiry, do not challenge the Trump effect immediately and forcefully, then soon the primary rhetorical skills our students will bring to our classrooms will be inciting xenophobia, retreating into isolationism, resorting to shouting, causing disruption, spouting insults, securing exclusion, encouraging divisiveness, spewing invective, exploiting fear, and desiring success at all costs. These unethical qualities of rhetoric will be what our students see every day, and they will see that they work. This is a rhetorical ecology in which I do not want to teach.

I believe that we need to confront post-truth rhetoric head-on. Bullshit must be held to a standard of evidence that it cannot survive. Fake news must be held to a standard of truth that it cannot withstand. Ethos and pathos at the expense of logos must be held to a standard of reasoning that they cannot endure. And the Trump effect must be countered with ethical rhetorical standards that prevent the future development of bullshit, fake news, and ethos and pathos at the expense of logos. Although I do not have space in this essay to explore specific pedagogical strategies for teaching ethical rhetoric and challenging unethical post-truth rhetoric, I hope that I have at least started the process of thinking in that direction. Writing is power, and teaching writing requires a deep sense of responsibility. It is our responsibility to check and counter the effects of post-truth rhetoric as quickly and as strongly as we can. The fate of our discipline is at hand, and that's not bullshit.

Notes

1. Clark's statement (available at https://associationdatabase.com/aws/RSA
/pt/sd/news_article/130762/_PARENT/layout_details/false) follows:

> As we emerge from a long and rancorous national election season, it seems
> appropriate to reaffirm that the Rhetoric Society of America stands for
> diversity, inclusion, and respect for all. Above all, we value the ongoing
> project of listening to each other in our diversity and engaging our differ-
> ences with mutual respect whether among our members, those who par-
> ticipate in our programs, or those who work with us in documenting and
> analyzing rhetoric. At a time when political rhetoric has been so divisive, it
> is important for us to come together around the values we share as a society
> with a scholarly mission to advance responsible discourse.

2. This statement is available on the CWPA website (at http://wpacouncil
.org/node/7535). Miller-Cochran's message follows:

> The Council of Writing Program Administrators is committed to ensur-
> ing a diverse, inclusive, and supportive environment in which WPAs, the
> instructors in the programs they direct, and the students in those pro-
> grams can continue to thrive and learn. Consequently, we are committed
> to explicitly acting against any programs, policies, or other structures in
> society and schools that produce inequality, division, exclusion, or unfair
> advantage to any one group by luck of birth.
>
> During the 2016 Presidential election, we heard harsh rhetoric that
> caused great concern among many of those in our community. Since the
> election of Donald Trump as President, we have seen violence and other
> hate-inspired acts on our campuses and elsewhere that make members
> of our community fear for their safety and futures. This election has also
> called our core values into question: diversity and inclusiveness have been
> part of CWPA's research and administrative agendas since the forming of
> the organization. We have also recently started a more targeted effort to
> diversify the membership of the CWPA Executive Board, its committees,
> and the organization as a whole. What we know about how students
> learn to write, and how we might design programs to support that, is in-
> formed by those students' ethnicities, genders, classes, sexual orientations,
> abilities, religions, and languages; what WPAs from diverse backgrounds

bring to us is a more informed and richly nuanced perspective that is invaluable to all of us, but particularly to the students in our programs. We also know that building a more just and equitable world in the future means explicitly confronting the structural problems that cause our society to be racist, sexist, ableist, homophobic, monolingualist, among other problems of injustice. So we continue to pledge to identify such problems and act against them.

CWPA pledges to continue its diversity effort and will also continue to foster inclusion more generally; promote research into student diversities; promote policies that increase diversity in our membership and in the population of people who administer writing programs; and explicitly act against the structures that cause injustice today. We will continue to work with reasonable parties to achieve acceptable policy compromises that honor all the lives, backgrounds, and learning conditions of our students. However, we will also continue to oppose the adoption of national, state, and university policies that harm the diverse students who learn to write in our programs, the diverse instructors who teach in our programs, and the diverse WPAs who administer those programs, and we will work to change those policies already in place.

3. This "Statement on Language, Power, and Action" (available at http://www .ncte.org/cccc/language-power-action) was later re-sent only to CCCC members through the CCCC listserv in case members did not find it in their *NCTE Inbox* email. The CCCC "Statement on Language, Power, and Action" follows:

Writing is powerful. It empowers individuals to explore and change themselves and their worlds. A belief in this power of writing and the ability of writers is at the core of CCCC's beliefs.

The recent election provided examples of writing being used to disempower and demean. In light of these events, CCCC reaffirms its commitments to cultivating writers, to teaching and research, and to classrooms that engage the full range of the power and potential of writers and writing. Acting on these commitments requires respect for diversity, equity, social justice, and intellectual and pedagogical freedom.

CCCC is proud to support its members, who every day engage writers from all backgrounds and cultures to explore how writing can be used to foster responsible and respectful inquiry and discussion across a range of contexts. In this contentious climate, we stand strongly for the use of fact-based reasoning, writing, and communication to build a better, more ethical, more engaged nation.

4. Though it is less directly relevant to my discussion here, the Modern Language Association also distributed and published a response to the 2016 campaign and election rhetoric (available at https://www.mla.org/About-Us/Governance /Executive-Council/Executive-Council-Actions/2016/MLA-Statement-on-the-2016-Presidential-Election).

5. Other contenders for word of the year in 2016 were *adulting*, *alt-right*, *Brexiteer*, *chatbot*, *coulrophobia*, *hygge*, *Latinx*, and *woke* (Oxford Dictionaries 2016).

6. Fundamentally, bullshit is a lack of concern with truth and reality, but that does not mean it is always wrong. Frankfurt (2005) writes: "[A]lthough [bullshit] is produced without concern with the truth, it need not be false. The bullshitter is faking things. But this does not mean that he necessarily gets them wrong" (47–48). Bullshit may be right or it may be wrong (or it may fall somewhere in between); the point is that the bullshitting rhetor just doesn't care.

7. For a series of case studies in rhetoric and bullshit, see the forum on the subject in *Rhetoric Society Quarterly* (2015) that includes short essays by Jenny Rice, Patricia Roberts-Miller, Anna M. Young, Jaime L. Wright, and Eric Detweiler and Joshua Gunn (Rice 2015; Roberts-Miller 2015; Young 2015; Wright 2015; Detweiler and Gunn 2015). Philip Eubanks and John D. Schaeffer (2008) apply bullshit to the writing that academics and students do.

8. I refer throughout this section to the transcript of the speech printed in *The Washington Post* on June 16, 2015 (Trump 2015).

References

Boston, Rob. 2016. "Humanists and the Rise of 'Post-Truth America.'" *The Humanist*, January–February, 32–33. Academic Search Premier, accession number 111887460.

Costello, Maureen B. 2016. "The Trump Effect: The Impact of the 2016 Presidential Election on Our Nation's Schools." Southern Poverty Law Center. November 28. http://www.splcenter.org/20161128/trump-effect-impact -2016-presidential-election-our-nations-schools.

Council of Writing Program Administrators. 2014. *WPA Outcomes Statement for First-Year Composition (v3.0)*, adopted July 17. http://www.wpacouncil.org /positions/outcomes.html.

Council of Writing Program Administrators, National Council of Teachers of English, and National Writing Project. 2011. *Framework for Success in Postsecondary Writing*. http://www.wpacouncil.org/files/framework-for-suc cess-postsecondary-writing.pdf.

Decker, Cathleen, and Michael A. Memoli. 2016. "Fake News but a Very Real Danger; An Online Conspiracy Theory Inspires an Armed Man to Show Up at a Washington Pizza Parlor." *Los Angeles Times*, December 6, A5. LexisNexis Academic.

Detweiler, Eric, and Joshua Gunn. 2015. "A Petulant Demand." *Rhetoric Society Quarterly* 45:481–85. doi:10.1080/02773945.2015.1088339.

Dewey, Caitlin. 2016. "The Story a News Faker Never Imagined." *The Washington Post*, November 18, C1. LexisNexis Academic.

Dvorak, Petula. 2016. "When Spreading Fake News Leads to Real Consequences." *The Washington Post*, December 6, B2. LexisNexis Academic.

Eubanks, Philip, and John D. Schaeffer. 2008. "A Kind Word for Bullshit: The Problem of Academic Writing." *College Composition and Communication* 59:372–88. http://www.jstor.org/stable/20457010.

"Fake News, Real Gunfire." 2016. Editorial. *The Washington Post*, December 7, A18. LexisNexis Academic.

Frankfurt, Harry G. 2005. *On Bullshit*. Princeton, NJ: Princeton University Press.

Fredal, James. 2011. "Rhetoric and Bullshit." *College English* 73:243–59. http://www.jstor.org/stable/25790474.

Heer, Jeet. 2015. "Donald Trump Is Not a Liar, He's Something Worse: A Bullshit Artist." *New Republic*, December 1. https://newrepublic.com/article /124803/donald-trump-not-liar.

Kristof, Nicholas. 2016. "Lies in Guise of News in the Trump Era." *The New York Times*, November 13, SR11. LexisNexis Academic.

Lombardo, Cara. 2016. "Deconstructing the Rightwing Spin Machine." *The Progressive*, February, 19–21. LexisNexis Academic.

Marcus, Ruth. 2016. "Post-Truth, It's All-Fake." *The Washington Post*, December 14, A17. LexisNexis Academic.

McAdams, Dan P. 2016. "The Mind of Donald Trump." *The Atlantic* (June): 76–90. Reader's Guide Full Text Mega.

Milbank, Dana. 2016. "Trump's Fake News Presidency." *The Washington Post*, November 20, A17. LexisNexis Academic.

Miller, Cassie, and Alexandra Werner-Winslow. 2016. "Ten Days After: Harassment and Intimidation in the Aftermath of the Election." Southern Poverty Law Center. November 29. http://www.splcenter.org/20161129/ten-days-after-harassment-and-intimidation-aftermath-election.

Morris, Brogan. 2016. "Trump's Lies Aren't Unique to America: Post-Truth Politics Are Killing Democracies on Both Sides of the Atlantic." *Salon*, June 19. http://www.salon.com/2016/06/19/trumps_lies_arent_unique_to_america_post_truth_politics_are_killing_democracies_on_both_sides_of_the_atlantic/.

Murphy, Katharine. 2016. "Don't Blame the Media: Trumpland Is a Place Where Truth Doesn't Matter." *The Guardian*, November 10. https://theguardian.com/australia-news/2016/nov/11/dont-blame-the-media-trumpland-is-a-place-where-truth-doesnt-matter.

O'Neil, Luke. 2016. "Pizzagate Is Just the Latest Sign We're Living in a Post-Truth Dystopia." *Esquire,* December 5. http://www.esquire.com/news-politics/news/a51255/pizzagate-conspiracy-theories-post-truth/.

Oxford Dictionaries. 2016. "Word of the Year 2016 Is . . . Post-Truth." Oxford Dictionaries. https://en.oxforddictionaries.com/word-of-the-year/word-of-the-year-2016.

Paresh, Dave. 2016. "Ads Are Key to Making Money in Fake News." *Los Angeles Times*, December 11, C1. LexisNexis Academic.

Rabin-Havt, Ari. 2016. *Lies, Incorporated: The World of Post-Truth Politics*. New York: Anchor Books.

Rice, Jenny. 2015. "Disgusting Bullshit." *Rhetoric Society Quarterly* 45:468–72. doi:10.1080/02773945.2015.1088339.

Roberts-Miller, Patricia. 2015. "Conspiracy Bullshit." *Rhetoric Society Quarterly* 45:464–67. doi:10.1080/02773945.2015.1088339.

Smith, Justin E. H. 2016. "Truth after Trump: Lies, Memes, and the Alt-Right." *The Chronicle Review*, November 4, B4–B5. http://chronicle.texterity.com/chronicle/20161104b?pg=4#pg4.

Southern Poverty Law Center. 2016. "The Trump Effect: The Impact of the Presidential Campaign on Our Nation's Schools." Southern Poverty Law

Center. April 13. http://www.splcenter.org/20160413/trump-effect-im
pact-presidential-campaign-our-nations-schools.

Tallis, Benjamin. 2016. "Living in Post-Truth: Power/Knowledge/Responsibility."
New Perspectives 24 (1): 7–18. http://ceenewperspectives.iir.cz/wp-con
tent/uploads/2016/07/1.NP_2016_01_Tallis_Editorial_Living_in_Post
Truth-1.pdf.

Tate, Amelia. 2016. "Facebook's False Reality: Why Fake Political News Is on the
Rise." *New Statesman*, September 9, 17. Social Sciences Full Text, accession
number 117973830.

Trump, Donald. 2015. "Donald Trump Announces a Presidential Bid." Full Text
Transcript of a Speech Delivered in New York, NY, June 16, 2015. *The
Washington Post*, June 16. https://www.washingtonpost.com/news/post
-politics/wp/2015/06/16/donald-trump-to-announce-his-presidential
-plans-today/?utm_term=.92e3e255dcfb.

Viner, Katharine. 2016. "How Technology Disrupted the Truth." *The Guardian*,
July 12. http://theguardian.com/media/2016/jul/12/how-technology-dis
rupted-the-truth.

Wright, Jaime L. 2015. "Adjudication Bullshit." *Rhetoric Society Quarterly* 45:476–
81. doi: 10.1080/02773945.2015.1088339.

"Yes, I'd Lie to You: The Post-Truth World." 2016. *The Economist*, September 10,
17–20. http://www.economist.com/node/21706498/print.

Young, Anna M. 2015. "The Politics of Wine and the Style of Bullshit." *Rhetoric
Society Quarterly* 45:472–75. doi:10.1080/02773945.2015.1088339.

About the Author

Bruce McComiskey is professor of rhetoric and composition and director of professional writing in the English Department at the University of Alabama at Birmingham. He is the author of *Dialectical Rhetoric*, *Gorgias and the New Sophistic Rhetoric*, and *Teaching Composition as a Social Process*. He is also the editor of *English Studies: An Introduction to the Discipline(s)* and *Microhistories of Composition* and coeditor of *City Comp: Identities, Spaces, Practices*.

Current Arguments in Composition

Utah State University Press's Current Arguments in Composition is a series of short-form publications of provocative original material and selections from foundational titles by leading thinkers in the field. Perfect for the composition classroom as well as the professional collection, this series provides access to important introductory content as well as innovative new work intended to stimulate scholarly conversation. Volumes are available in paperback or ebook form.